The Lost
Back-to-Back
Streets of Leeds

The Lost
Back-to-Back
Streets of Leeds

Woodhouse in the 1960s and '70s

Colin and Elizabeth James

The
History
Press

First published 2024
The History Press
97 St George's Place, Cheltenham,
Gloucestershire, GL50 3QB
www.thehistorypress.co.uk

British Library Cataloguing in Publication Data.
A catalogue record for this book is available from the British Library.

ISBN 978 1 80399 514 4

Typesetting and origination by The History Press
Printed and bound in Great Britain by TJ Books Limited, Padstow, Cornwall.

Trees for LYfe

Contents

Colin James has been an active photographer since he acquired his first camera at the age of 12. He began taking photographs in Leeds as a student at the University studying for a food science MSc, (1967-69). His career was spent in the food industry and latterly in school but his first love is photography and he rarely leaves home in King's Lynn without a camera! Some of his pictures have appeared in magazines and other publications, plus requests from local organisations for event pictures to be submitted to the local press.

Elizabeth James read Latin at the University of Leeds (1967-70) and also holds an MA in local and regional history from the University of East Anglia (1991). She is a retired administrator of King's Lynn Minster, and formerly a curator of the Lynn Museum. Her first love is local buildings and heritage but whatever she studies is rooted in the lives of the people at the heart of it. Alongside working on Leeds with Colin, she collaborated with a friend on a book publishing over seventy songs collected in Lynn by Ralph Vaughan Williams in 1905, for which she researched the lives of the individual local singers.

Foreword

I was really pleased to have been recommended by Leeds Civic Trust to write the foreword for this book. As I found out during the course of my MA and PhD research on back-to-back houses in the Harehills neighbourhood of Leeds, my twenty-year connection with the houses is not a long one – I met some residents and former residents whose family had lived in a single house for around eighty years. I only lived in mine for five, but there was something about them that fascinated me, and I've spent the last ten years doing the same things as Colin and Elizabeth have in producing this book – trekking the streets with my camera and survey forms, trawling through archives, and trying to piece together the architectural and social history. There is a lot of interest throughout Leeds in the back-to-back houses, demonstrated not just to me as a researcher, but to Leeds Library and Leeds Museums, who have reported on the popularity of my guest blogs and exhibitions. But interest is wider than that, evidenced by the success of my academic articles and my TV appearance on *Great British Railway Journeys*.

In Harehills, developed from 1888, most of the streets are still extant, but I led a community project in 2021 that was a spin-off of my main research. Entitled 'Rediscovering the lost streets of Victorian Burmantofts and Sheepscar', I couldn't help smiling when I saw the title of this book. These two neighbourhoods comprised predominantly Victorian terraced houses, but the houses and most of the streets were lost to so-called slum clearance. The designs, and I expect also the social history of these earlier houses, have much in common with those in Woodhouse featured in this book.

The importance of the history and heritage captured in this book cannot be overstated. The houses and shops may be lost on the ground, they may be lost in the memories of younger generations, and they may not even be known to newcomers, but now we have a comprehensive collection of photographs that can be passed on and remembered. What is also of significance in this work is that the period of the photography was one of rapid transition between the Victorian and Edwardian way of life and the modernity that we now have.

My own research indicated that despite the back-to-backs having more sophisticated facilities than similar-sized houses in other towns at the turn of the twentieth century, they did not change much at all until the government-initiated improvement programmes of the 1960s, '70s and '80s. Colin and Elizabeth report much the same in Woodhouse.

Another important insight, again replicated in the Harehills research, is the way in which residents of back-to-back houses complied with the same social norms as their counterparts in small through terraces, for example by washing clothes in the kitchen and hanging it on a line to dry. It seems obvious enough, but adaptations were made to achieve this, most notably, hanging washing across the street rather than in a back yard.

Colin and Elizabeth are astute in their selection of quotes and their observations, showing the many facets of a declining neighbourhood and the concerns of residents awaiting relocation prior to demolition of their houses. These themes are evident in other research too; not just in Leeds's twentieth-century history, but more recently in Liverpool's Welsh Streets, where residents suffered at the hands of the government's Housing Market Renewal Programme, aka 'Pathfinder'.

The final chapter ensures that this is not just another local history book. Moving into discussion of architectural conservation and separating cosmetic or service deficiencies from the structural integrity and heritage value of the houses, it adds to the growing literature on the relevance of older working-class housing for twenty-first-century living and the value it brings to our neighbourhoods.

This book will undoubtedly be of interest to current and former residents of Leeds, but also to historians, architects, planners and policy-makers throughout the UK who may look to it to fill a void in knowledge so they can learn from the past and develop their own work. Working in all of these fields, it is a book I shall keep close at hand.

Dr Joanne Harrison

Introduction

Books about local history based on old photographs are often a collection from several sources, but not this one. These pictures were taken in the 1960s and '70s, by one photographer, who is joint-author of this book. His fellow author has written the text, and we believe that the photographs have become an archive of an important period in the changing Leeds suburban landscape. Our book's aim is to share a selection of the pictures; it is our contribution to the records of the city where we met, while we were students at the University of Leeds.

Colin arrived from London and I from Norwich in the autumn of 1967. We found Leeds a very interesting city, full of friendly people but undergoing rapid changes. During that term my mother sent me a four-page feature on Leeds, dated 13 November 1967, from the *Daily Mirror*'s 'Boom Cities!' series.[1] Full of enthusiasm for change, progress and explosive economy, it highlighted the sweeping redevelopment of city centre buildings and suburban housing alike. The university, embarking on its own wave of major rebuilding, was described as 'a hotch-potch of ancient villas, stone blocks and holes in the ground'. That was sweeping journalism; we also had the venerable Waterhouse buildings in University Road and the lofty white Parkinson clocktower, reminding students of lecture times and regulating the neighbours' timepieces. But the *Mirror* feature also referred to back-to-back terraced housing, empty in expectation of the arrival of new houses, where 'cobbled streets sprout grass, corner shops are shuttered. A gas lamp lights no footsteps.'

Colin was and is a keen photographer and he brought his cameras to his new home on campus. Just across Woodhouse Lane (the A660) he discovered the streets of back-to-back terraced housing. Despite what journalists chose to highlight, the gas lamps in Woodhouse still had work to do because the streets were not empty of life. Some houses were boarded up but many – often next door – were still family homes, albeit in the last years of occupation. Shops were still open, the washing lines swung in the wind across the streets where the children were playing, the cats and dogs sunbathed on doorsteps. They were a fertile source for Colin's photographs because there was nothing like them back home.

Publishing a selection of the pictures was the result of a chance suggestion by friends, who saw them as an archive to be shared with a wider audience. To help us select pictures and identify the right narrative theme for them we had two vital resources: the detailed photographic lists Colin had maintained at the time and the survival of our 1960s street atlas of Leeds. So many streets had vanished: their successors often perpetuate the venerable names of their predecessors, but they do not always follow the same layout on the ground. We loitered on street corners looking puzzled, map in hand, sometimes approached by helpful passers-by who thought we might be lost!

Much supporting research was needed for the text; we now live in Norfolk but it was a good excuse for repeated, if sporadic, visits to Leeds to carry it out. We needed to explore the rise of Victorian and Edwardian housing in Woodhouse and even to find out why the houses were built that way in the first place. Whose were the names above the shops? What did the residents think about the great 1960s clearance and rebuilding and where they would be living next? What was said to them about why it was thought necessary? Come to that, who decided it was necessary and why?

We received very generous help to find the answers from people who sometimes went the extra mile in doing so and they are named with gratitude in the formal acknowledgements. At such a distance we still do not feel qualified to write an exhaustive account of how one area of the city among many went through such a transformation; our narrative focuses on the story as told by the pictures themselves.

In addition to Woodhouse itself, Colin also took interesting pictures of the terraces just above Burley Road, technically part of 'Little Woodhouse', and at Burley itself, which it seemed a shame not to include. We have also included some well-chosen present-day photographs to provide clarity, add extra information and help to show good things that came out of the redevelopment: pleasant houses and wide green recreational spaces where there were none before.

All buildings are shaped by the needs, whether or not well-met, of the people who have lived or worked in them. People appear in many of these photographs because a good photographer knows that they bring a picture to life. The November 1967 *Daily Mirror* feature quoted that year's Lord Mayor of Leeds, Colonel Lawrence Turnbull, saying: 'Leeds is Leeds because of the people who live in it.' And that is why we have such happy memories of being part of it.

Elizabeth James, June 2023

Technical Notes

Colin had two cameras, a Pentax SV with standard 55mm lens, and a Nikkormat with 35 and 105mm lenses. Most of the pictures are black and white photographs from 35mm negatives using Ilford FP4 or Kodak Tri X and Plus X films, processed using the darkroom facilities in the students' union. The colour pictures were taken on Kodachrome 25 and 64 slide film, largely in the autumn term of 1967 and after 1970. Recent comparative pictures are digital photographs taken on a Nikon D800.

April 1970: Danube Terrace, Leeds 12. Reading the sports page of the *Yorkshire Evening Post*. The contemporary local newspapers were a valuable source for research.

Chapter 1

The Back-to-Back Houses of Leeds and Why they Started to Disappear [1]

In the eighteenth century, the main streets of most old towns were lined with long narrow plots running back from the shops and dwellings fronting the street. Where industrialisation led to greater housing needs, the first move was to fill up these rear yards with little dwellings; in Leeds this infill focused on plots off Kirkgate, Briggate and the Headrow. By 1800 those cramped spaces were full and over the next century, to meet the ever-expanding need, development spread out from the city in all directions. This book, however, focuses particularly on the spread north-west between the River Aire and the Meanwood Beck. Among the first areas to be engulfed there were Carlton Hill and Sheepscar and, in due course, Woodhouse.

In 1961 Maurice W Beresford, Professor of Economic History at the University, devoted much of his inaugural lecture to the transformation of Woodhouse, where some of the earliest cottages consisted only of 'one room up-one down', sometimes with a separate cellar dwelling below. Available land plots were snapped up piecemeal but tended at first to be fairly small, which sometimes gave rise to 'half streets', perhaps ending in a wall, and odd changes in level.[2] One of Beresford's examples showed how a particular group of streets was laid out between 1874 and 1882 on old fields, linked by a road along one of the field boundaries. Later slumps in business prevented extensions across it onto an adjoining plot until 1898–1901.[3] This group included Livinia, Claypit, Prosperity, Hawkins and Kenealy Streets, some of which appear in photographs in later chapters.

Unbroken rows of back-to-back terraces was the initial norm, unless the gradient made a double row in the block impracticable or because it was hoped to acquire more land later, which sometimes never happened. Resulting single rows would have a mono-pitched roof up to an unbroken back wall and were termed 'blind backs'.

By 1860 the brick-and-mortar carpet was heading for Roundhay, Potter Newton, Chapel Allerton and Headingley, but larger fields there enabled better planning. Some former estate lands were becoming available: the Earl of Cardigan's former estate will be mentioned later in connection with Burley but was extensive enough also to meet up with the side of Woodhouse Moor. Planned groups of streets often included a 'Street', 'Terrace', 'View', 'Grove' etc, sharing a single given name, such as 'Servia', or 'Herbert'. Our chapters will follow the convenient practice of referring to such groups as the 'Servias' or the 'Herberts' when describing the local topography.

'Back-to-back' terraces were causing concern on health grounds as early as 1842. Building only in blocks of eight (i.e. four backing on to four) with space between for privies was suggested but dictation to landowners of what they should build on their own land was unwelcome and for now the suggestion was shelved.[4] Other cities, however, were soon pressing for a privy and ash pit *per house* and passing byelaws aimed at preventing more back-to-backs being built at all. In Leeds back-to-back building continued for many more decades, but in due course a byelaw did indeed pick up the suggestion of building in blocks of eight instead of long uninterrupted terraces, and the pattern became a common Leeds hallmark after 1870. The shared toilets for the blocks were placed with an ash pit in intervening yards that later accommodated the dustbin as well.

Houses in a 'four by four' block pattern were usually double fronted, with the living room and a scullery either side of the front door, two bedrooms and an attic above and a coal cellar below. Probably most of the terraces surviving in the late 1960s, and indeed today, were of this standard type. The separate scullery improved upon a kitchen that had often occupied a cellar. Nevertheless, surveyors making pre-redevelopment inspections not infrequently found traces of an old cellar kitchen, even if not still in use. They also noted with distaste the shared toilet, sometimes entered by a dark and narrow passage directly from the street, as in this 1960 compulsory purchase order: 'Sanitary accommodation used in common and not readily accessible is unjustifiable on any ground, but on the ground of health is utterly indefensible.'[5]

An alternative pattern provided a back-to-back terrace where one row faced not onto another street but onto a shared yard, to which the front-facing houses had access via passages. The shared 'facilities' opened onto this yard, not the street, and the washing hung there as well. Evidence for this pattern in Leeds is scant on the old maps, certainly in our area, but such a terrace does appear on the Ordnance Survey's 1949 edition in Scott Street, just off Woodhouse Street. Scott Street was declared an 'unhealthy area' in 1954[6], and the Holborn Tower block of flats was built on its site in 1965. Stockdale Terrace, on Institution Street, was also of this type and survived long enough to appear in a photograph in Chapter 2. A Bradford terrace of this type was rebuilt at the Bradford Industrial Museum, where you can explore it today. Its houses are only 'one room up and one down' and if that was the case in Scott Street it would have made it a priority case for demolition. The National Trust's preserved back-to-back houses in Birmingham are not unlike this layout.

After 1890 the long unbroken terrace returned, but with an individual toilet and wash house per house. In time section 43 of the 1909 Town Planning Act banned back-to-back building but left a loophole in the legislation: if the plans had been approved by a council before 1 May 1909 they could be put into effect. This clause was called upon over an extraordinarily elastic time span, because of the breaks in building during the First World War and its economic aftermath during the 1920s. The last Leeds back-to-backs were built as late as 1937.

Ironically by now the 1930 Housing Act had come into force to encourage the clearing of slums as a high priority. Attention in Leeds fell initially on the earliest, poorest-quality and most densely packed houses: the 1933 'Woodhouse Street Unhealthy Areas Clearance Order' reveals some houses consisting of only one room in total, perhaps old cellar dwellings, or with only one room downstairs.[7] These houses seem to have been on Woodhouse Street itself, once the original 'village' street, and could well have been the earliest. Forty-seven out of eighty-five were in enclosed yards or courts. Some were reached by approaches 'so narrow as to be almost inaccessible' and some seemed to have 'almost complete absence of light and air'. Four courts were singled out by name: 'These places are entered through narrow passages … the surfaces are uneven, or unpaved, and the flagging defective, leaving hollows in which in wet weather the surface water stands and becomes foul.' The 'decayed, damp, dark and poorly ventilated' houses frequently had 'no facilities for household washing, the sinks are defective' and they had 'no proper provision for the storage of food'. Compared with these the later back-to-backs in their blocks of eight sound like little palaces, but their turn was to come later.

Rehousing the displaced residents had to be taken into the equation. Redevelopment of the Quarry Hill area immediately east of the city centre resulted in the former Quarry Hill flats scheme.[8] This complex of 938 flats (built 1935–41, demolished 1976–78) was the largest comprehensive development of social housing in the country, perhaps inspired by similar large-scale schemes on the Continent (see page 24). The plan included shops, laundry, community hall and other facilities to serve the residents, although in fact not all were built. Its huge semicircular, convex frontage towards Eastgate was noted as 'forbidding' by Pevsner, who dubbed it the 'Chinese Wall'[9], but the flats themselves were roomy and were remembered with affection by former residents after its demolition. In 1976 we eavesdropped on a conversation between a former resident and a workman: the ex-resident paid tribute to a comfortable flat; the workman to reinforced concrete very difficult to demolish!

Many displaced householders, especially from the pre-1870 back-to-backs, were rehoused on new but more peripheral estates at Gipton and elsewhere, necessarily built where land was available, while the sites of the old houses awaited rebuilding after clearance.

The Second World War halted slum clearance schemes and also created its own major housing shortage. The government made housing and slum clearance a major 1950s welfare priority, heralded by the 1954 Housing (Repairs and Rent) Act and accelerated by the 1957 Housing Act. The strict housing standards were particularly strong on bathrooms and sanitation and front to back through ventilation, making back-to-back houses an obvious target.

A Housing Area Map for Leeds was prepared in 1962, which appears to be the undated map we saw in the West Yorkshire Archives.[10] It is based on the 'City of Leeds Central Smoke Control Area' with a new key, listing no fewer than eight different types of clearance, including confirmed and proposed slum clearances, plus areas that had been cleared already. Woodhouse features prominently, almost entirely as 'Dwelling houses to be dealt with under the Housing (Financial Provisions) Act 1958'.

A total of 22,500 houses, mainly back-to-backs, were to be cleared and redeveloped in the city over the next ten years.[11] Some 20,000 more could be upgraded temporarily with grant-aided modern amenities but with strong emphasis on 'temporarily'. The smaller bedroom could become a bathroom and a huge attic dormer, such a prominent feature of many surviving back-to-backs, would create a new attic bedroom, to create a fifteen-year respite, while broadly satisfying the Housing Act. Later pre-redevelopment surveys show grant offers were taken up with enthusiasm, and home owners had supplemented them with their own cash input. Fifteen years sounded a long way off but the axe was still poised, not withdrawn.

With plans drawn up on a major timescale for the provision of new homes, on estates or in tower blocks, and the strategic moving of huge numbers of people into them, redevelopment got under way. It was accepted that it would take years to complete but as time went on each area of rebuilding was available to accommodate the residents of the next and so on. Over the years many unforeseen events and circumstances could and did crop up to create not just delays but fresh considerations. Nevertheless, however we regard the effects of such a draconian scheme today, it is only fair to pay tribute to those with the commitment and courage to take it on, bearing in mind that it was happening not just in Woodhouse but all round the city.

1969: North West Grove, a 'blind back' below St Mark's Road: The 'toothing' in of the brickwork would have helped key in a further row of houses, which were never built. Valuations of 1886–87 show that the 'North Wests' were standing by that date.[12]

Clockwise from above:

August 1968: Hawkins Place:
Looking towards the Carlton Croft
tower block on the corner of Carlton
Street and Oatland Lane. The streets
on the left were laid out on an old field
up to Hawkins Place, which was one
of the field boundaries.[13]

1969: Toilet and ash pit shelter in Well
Close Road: An entrance direct from
the public pavement to shared sanitary
accommodation was seen as highly
unsatisfactory by surveyors.[14]

April 1970: Danube Terrace, Leeds
12: This striking shot through 'toilet
gaps', straight across three of the
'Danubes', shows that sometimes the
gap was much wider.

October 1969: Woodhouse Street: Midgley Square was one of four courts or yards here singled out by name in 1933 as insanitary. Ironically it may have stood on – and even incorporated – the site of the old manor house. It was replaced by this neat 1930s development, whose shops now face directly onto Woodhouse Street.

Opposite page:

Top: **1969:** Building details in Leicester Mount: Terraces often included some nice decorative details, here emphasised by the gable shadows from a dormer window across the road. The little cast iron coal hole cover catches the light.

Bottom: **November 1972:** Back Eldon Street: The picture highlights the distinctive textures of this area: the worn brick, stone flags and square setts.

April 1970: Thirteenth Avenue in Armley. Most back-to-back developments consisted of Street, Terrace, Grove, Place etc with a single identifying name. In this development off Tong Road in Armley, eighteen streets around a school were simply numbered! New houses still cluster round the school and preserve the names First, Second and Eighth Avenue.

July 1970: The Quarry Hill flats, demolished 1976. Its convex exterior was considered 'forbidding' from outside by Pevsner and Colin admits to finding it daunting to enter; but the concave curve sheltering its court had a much gentler aspect and former residents have recorded happy memories.[15]

April 1970: off Oatland Road. This area had been cleared in the early 1960s.[16] The backs of Meanwood Road properties run across the middle of the picture and behind are the tower blocks of flats off Stoney Rock Lane in Burmantofts.

May 1970: Demolition in Grant Row off Roundhay Road. The signboard shows that the city council was in charge of the demolition.

November 1972: The junction of Sheepscar Road North and Chapeltown Road. Land clearances made possible major 'improvements' to the road system. This sharp-angled fork is now part of a complex multi-lane junction and you certainly don't stand there to take a photograph. JA Watson (butcher), responsible for the pun painted on the wall, was trading in 1955.

May 1970: Mount Preston, on the edge of the university campus. Demolition could be a summary procedure and it was not only the smaller houses that suffered it in the 1970s. This one was just off Clarendon Road. This series shows the method sometimes used of putting a cable around the building and pulling with a heavy vehicle. The bystanders are surprisingly close and the phone box even more so!

And all that remains is to clear up what's left.

Chapter 2

Exploring 'Great' Woodhouse and its History

Woodhouse had not always been an area of densely packed terraced streets; it began life as a small village a few miles outside the city. Professor Beresford correctly refers to it below as 'Great' Woodhouse, to distinguish it from its small outlier on the other side of Woodhouse Moor, but the map of the Borough of Leeds published by Messrs Baines and Newsome in 1834[1] calls it simply 'Woodhouse'. This fascinating map goes beyond Leeds itself to show Woodhouse and many other small hamlets, outlying communities before streets of houses united them with the city (see page 33). Woodhouse Moor forms a prominent quadrilateral easily spotted on the west side of Woodhouse Lane, which still passes over it as the A660, en route to Headingley and beyond; Woodhouse itself lies to the east of it. Opposite the north-east corner of the moor, the road is joined by Woodhouse Street, once the village's main artery.

North of the street, beyond a cluster of houses, open land ran up to the crest of Woodhouse Ridge, whose steeply wooded scarp overlooks Meanwood Beck valley, through which Meanwood Road runs towards the city. The municipal authorities took possession of Woodhouse Moor in 1855 to create a park for the ever-expanding city,[2] and in 1876 they also acquired leafy Woodhouse Ridge.[3] By 1850 the sloping land up to the top of it was being used for quarrying stone, which would one day have serious consequences for houses built there. This area forms the final chapter in this book; reaction in the late 1970s and '80s to its proposed redevelopment marked a milestone in the story of Woodhouse and its back-to-back houses.

In 1834, however, most of the houses appear on the opposite side of Woodhouse Street, below a corresponding slope up towards Woodhouse Moor and Woodhouse Lane. There, on what would later become St Mark's

Road, the map says proudly 'New Church'. In 1822–23 Woodhouse was awarded funding for a commissioners' church provided for under the Million Act of 1818. This Act, in thanksgiving for the end of the Napoleonic threat, provided £1 million to fund new churches in developing areas without one. Other nineteenth-century churches sprang up like mushrooms around Leeds, but only three – St Mark's Woodhouse, St Mary's Quarry Hill and Christ Church Meadow Lane – were commissioners' churches. Today St Mark's is the only survivor of the three. Even by the 1820s the old village justified a commissioners' church; perhaps already the old courts of tiny cramped dwellings, described there in horrific terms in 1933, were taking shape. In his lecture Professor Beresford referred to nineteenth-century artisan housing spreading 'into the quite remote hamlet of Great Woodhouse'.[4]

Above the church the land continues rising to Woodhouse Lane. Today St Mark's Road is L-shaped: the upper arm opens onto Woodhouse Lane, opposite today's university buildings, the lower arm past the church onto the foot of the moor, but before redevelopment the two did not quite join. They are still in separate postal districts.

The old village lay in the hollow between the moor and the slope up to the ridge, but Woodhouse Street's downhill course through it was relatively gentle. The later nineteenth-century developers, however, had no qualms about tackling the steeper hillsides of the Meanwood Beck valley between the village and the city, as a view of Woodhouse taken from the far side in 1970 shows very clearly on page 34. By 1900, no longer a village, Woodhouse had become a less focused area not so easy to grasp, while changes in the road pattern, brought about by twentieth-century redevelopment, have impacted further on the layout left by the Victorians.

The area covered by this chapter as 'Great' Woodhouse, to distinguish it from Little Woodhouse across the moor, is bounded to the south-west and north-east by Woodhouse Lane and Meanwood Road, converging towards the city, and to the north by Woodhouse Ridge: see plate 01 for the 1960s map in use when the photographs were taken. To the south a rough demarcation line before the city centre is made on the map by Claypit Lane. This has since been extended as a major dual carriageway and the route of the extension added for clarity. We have marked in yellow on the map the bus route from the bridge over Claypit Lane along Oatland Lane up to Woodhouse Street, along with the road up to St Mark's. These lines are a useful point of reference to which individual streets in the photographs can be related.

On the 1850 edition Ordnance Survey map, 'Oatland' just indicates a nearby house, a cloth mill on Meanwood Road and a bridge just beyond it over Meanwood Beck. Oatland Lane itself was then known as Camp Road, presumably because, as the map says, 'General Wade's Army camped here in 1745', a temporary camp at the time of the Jacobite Rebellion.[5]

The area between it and Meanwood Road is known as 'Little London' and the name already appears on OS 1850. Beresford refers briefly to it: bracketing early development into 'the quite remote hamlet' of Woodhouse with 'the isolated field on Carlton Hill that gave birth to Little London'.[6] On OS 1850 it is shown as a small, quite isolated set of streets with the appearance of a deliberate development, which by 1893 had been totally engulfed by later development.[7] Today the name is applied more generally to the area around Oatland Lane and its significant part in the area transformation justifies our inclusion of it in Woodhouse.

In 1850 Camp Road seems to have gone no further than General Wade's campsite. By 1893, however, a dotted line on the Ordnance Survey map marked a planned extension uphill to St Mark's Road: in 1906 this was known as New Camp Road but is now called Servia Hill. The 'Camp' names still featured on the 1960s street map used in this book (plate 01). However the current names Oatland Lane and Servia Hill were already in use as well: they appear in old street directories and indeed can be glimpsed on venerable name plates in two of the photographs (see page 39 and plate 22). It has seemed best to use those names in the chapters following, with a note under the map.

The two roads made no attempt to also link up with Woodhouse Street until Servia Road was laid out to connect them, flanked by the Servia, Claro and Wolseley terraces. The name perhaps followed the creation of the kingdom of Servia (Serbia) in 1882; in 1893 its terraces were still a work in progress, but complete by 1906. In addition, Cambridge Road approached at an angle from Meanwood Road, with its own sets of terraces alongside Servia Road. Both roads met on Woodhouse Street at the former Church of the Holy Name.[8]

Heading out of the city today therefore, a bus crosses over the Claypit Lane dual carriageway through 'Little London', whose back-to-back houses appear to have been among the first to go when housing redevelopment was revitalised. The map of clearance areas described in Chapter 1 shows much of it either cleared or facing clearance, up to and including General Wade's campsite. The 1960s street map also shows it empty, except for two little black squares at the bottom: two of the present three Lovell Park blocks of flats.

On the uphill side of Oatland Lane and Servia Hill, the rising ranks of roads and terraces, seen from across the Meanwood valley in that 1970 view from Chapeltown Road on page 34, would survive until the late 1960s and early '70s. From then onwards the view from the bus windows on the Oatland Lane to Woodhouse Street route would, increasingly, be changing all the time and gradually become very different.

The pictures in this chapter are arranged geographically, and chronologically only as a secondary consideration, as it is not always topographically practical. After the general view from Chapeltown Road, they begin in upper St Mark's Road above the church, then descend to the church, Servia Hill and its close neighbour Grosvenor Hill,[9] before following Servia Road and Cambridge Road to Woodhouse Street. Gradually you will become aware of the boarded-up windows becoming more prominent and discover the nuts and bolts of coping with ongoing dereliction as part of everyday life. This dereliction was often property by property and piecemeal, and it could be some time before demolition of a whole street could follow. These pictures are followed by the stark progress of pre-clearance dereliction on the hillside above Woodhouse Street and below St Mark's.

Empty houses might attract vandalism and squatters and, in due course, bring the local councillor May Sexton to look for herself and talk with anxious householders. Greatly interested in housing and welfare, in 1963 she caused a stir by phoning the city's acting welfare officer at 1 am, trying to arrange accommodation for three homeless people who had arrived on her doorstep.[10] In 1969 she met residents who were seriously disturbed by squatters in empty properties in Lomond Place (see page 54): incidents included drunkenness, brawls, gangs and threats to householders. But her concern included the welfare of the squatters as well, and led to a conversation with the head of a family of nine, including toddlers, living illicitly in one of the derelict houses.[11]

Excerpt from a map of the Borough of Leeds, published by Baines and Newsome in 1834, reproduced by kind permission of Leeds Libraries.

1970: Woodhouse from Chapeltown Road. The dark block with prominent chimneys on the extreme left is Ormonde Place on Meanwood Road, still there but without the chimneys. Behind it the Woodhouse terraces climb up to the university's Parkinson Tower on the skyline.

May 1970: Upper St Mark's Road, Bagby Terrace corner. The advertisement on the wall was already very old: William T Payne, painter, worked from 84 St Mark's Road, perhaps the little shop on the left, and lived at 8 Bagby Terrace in the 1940 and 1947 directories, but could not be found in 1955.

Spring 1970: off Kingston Road. Little sideways terraces off the steep hill down towards St Mark's church had nowhere for the usual washing line across the street, so the prop on the doorstep provided an alternative.

August 1968: Kingston Road. A small shop, probably a newsagent's.

May 1970: St Mark's Road. The church is immediately behind the viewer. The houses are probably in St Mark's Avenue, climbing up like Kingston Road. The retaining wall is still there but the new buildings are largely big student residence blocks and a sixth form college.

August 1996: St Mark's Church. Since 1996 the church stonework has been cleaned and the overgrown churchyard cleared: it is easier now to see its very interesting memorials.

August 1996: Looking up Servia Hill and St Mark's Road from the top of Grosvenor Hill. Servia Hill itself is almost invisible down below but runs past the tall building on the right and the Holborn tower block, a useful photographic landmark, built in 1965. The buildings on the left are on the site of Bray's Bagby Works factory, at which Grosvenor Hill ended.

May 1973: Servia Hill. Holborn Tower is further up on the right and the retaining wall stood against Grosvenor Hill. The road is too busy to string a washing line across, so the windowsill supports the prop.

May 1973: Servia Hill. Although so close together, Grosvenor Hill's gradient was much steeper, the difference shown by this flight of steps linking the two hills.

Summer 1970: The junction of Oatland Lane with Grosvenor Hill. The roads met at a very sharp angle but a pointed plot could not be wasted: a pointed house would be built instead! Built after 1893, OS 1906 tells us it was then a bank. Holborn Tower block on neighbouring St Mark's Road can just be glimpsed above the houses.

February 1972: Grosvenor Hill corner. Looking straight up Grosvenor Hill to the Bagby Works factory chimney, built for George Bray & Co. in 1943 and standing 154ft high.[12] Past the lamp post and telegraph pole to the right is Servia Road, where Servia Hill had its own sharp junction (see plate 22).

May 1970: Servia Road. A pair of corner shops in their last working years on the corners of Servia Street and Wolseley Terrace: the local butcher and newsagent.

Opposite: **May 1970:** This second set of steps leading up to Grosvenor Hill survives today (see plate 27). On the railing posts is cast 'W Horsfall & Co.'. Not a Leeds firm: they were based at Square Road, Halifax, in the 1894 and 1901 trade directories.

May 1970: Claro Grove, looking up to Servia Road from Cambridge Road. The gradual acquisition and boarding up of properties is unmistakeable.

July 1970: Cambridge Road. Cambridge and Servia Roads converged on Woodhouse Street. At least two of many end-terrace corner shops have been boarded up. The doorways show some nice moulded brick details.

1970: The 'North Wests' off Woodhouse Street, looking down from St Mark's Road. A stub of North West Road, which linked them, still boasts a name plate down on Woodhouse Street. Derelict toilets suggest replacement by grant-aided bathrooms in bedrooms. Leodis Student Residences now stand on their site.

May 1970: Craven Road off Woodhouse Street, opposite the 'North Wests'. Holborn Tower, up on St Mark's Road, forms a useful landmark. The 1969 telephone directory records Harris & Scully, whose name is on the signboard, as shopfitters at No. 11, formerly an engineering works.

May 1970: the Woodhouse Clothing Co. Ltd in Crowther Place off Woodhouse Street, in business in Kelly's Directory in 1966 but not mentioned in 1961. There were lots of small mills and factories scattered throughout Woodhouse, several were dye works and tanneries.

November 1968: Dereliction in Holborn Street. Just along Woodhouse Street from Craven Road and the 'North Wests', Holborn Street and its neighbour Institution Street, built by 1893, ran up behind and below St Mark's towards Woodhouse Moor. A major redevelopment scheme between Woodhouse Street and St Mark's Road began in 1967.[13] Holborn Street thereafter almost disappeared, bequeathing its name to several new 'Holborns'.

October 1969: Bloomfield Terrace. Above Holborn Street, Bloomfield Terrace ended at the wall of St Mark's churchyard. This little girl must have been living there, but the setts are grass-grown and, although the windows are not easy to see, there is a hint that the nearest one is broken and one further up is boarded.

October 1969: Institution Street. Dereliction is well advanced on the corner of Warren Terrace. Inside is an old coal-fired cooking range. Surveyors frequently reported an 'obsolete Yorkshire type range' still in use, although this seems to have been a shop. Sometimes they were unsafe: one in nearby Johnston Street had cracked oven plates and defective flue.[14]

October 1969: Institution Street. Another range, this time with the oven door in place, on the next corner with Armstrong Terrace. Rowland Lindup recalled with affection, 'What a feast of pies, tarts, buns, cakes, jam pasties and bread she [his mother] could produce from that small fireside oven!' But poor Mum had to work hard to keep it looking good and glowing, perhaps long before he was up.[15]

Opposite: **October 1968:** Stockdale Terrace, Institution Street. Now called Holborn Approach, Institution Street ran right up to Raglan Road below Woodhouse Moor. It was still at least partly occupied in October 1968, because the bath hangs outside one of the houses, but demolition at the top had started by February 1968 (see plate 10).

October 1969: Lucas Terrace, just off Woodhouse Street, with Midgley Terrace in the background. Two very small salvagers with a plank bigger than they are! The date is only a week before Bonfire Night. No back gardens but there was probably a big bonfire up on Woodhouse Moor. This looks like a floor joist, as glimpsed in the previous picture, with the floorboards already lying on the setts.

October 1969: Duxbury Place. It was in this month that nine Duxbury residents complained about vandalism in nearby empty houses.[16]

October 1969: Grosvenor Terrace, off Grosvenor Hill. The lads are having a good time exploring but as early as 1961 there were complaints elsewhere about tramps and youngsters getting into derelict houses; there were dangerous hazards, such as gaps where coal hole covers had been removed and broken glass.[17] Here the cellar has been bricked up but a tumble off that window sill might have made a sorry tale to take home to Mum.

October 1969: Lomond Street, looking down Hawkins Place towards the Little London tower blocks. The 'Lomonds' were too small to mark on the street map but were close to Grosvenor Terrace at the foot of Grosvenor Hill. Later that autumn Councillor May Sexton met with worried residents and squatters in Lomond Place[18]

1969: Clayfield Street. Keeping house (on the right) next to a derelict property (on the left). Clayfield Street was off Cambridge Road's neighbour Oxford Road, now a green area between Cambridge Road and Meanwood Road.

Chapter 3

Little Woodhouse and Burley

The high ground of Woodhouse Moor and Woodhouse Lane forms a 'watershed' between the Meanwood Beck Valley to the north-east and the major valley of the River Aire to the south-west. 'Little Woodhouse', across the Moor from its larger namesake, looks over towards the Aire. In the eighteenth century the historian Ralph Thoresby had described it as 'one of the pleasantest hamlets'[1] and it seems to have had an early social cachet not enjoyed by its larger neighbour. By 1800 it had attracted some large and elegant houses, some of which still survive. Some were built for the new city magnates whose mill chimneys were springing up down below by the Aire.

After Woodhouse Moor became a park in 1855, more big houses sprang up on Hyde Park Road and Moorland Road, which overlook two sides of it, and on Woodsley Road to the west (see plate 02). Woodsley and Hyde Park Roads converge at a point well down the Little Woodhouse hillside, forming a triangle just above the road from the city out to Burley. Here there was less lofty development and most of its interior had been flattened by 1967 (see plate 13). A large area on the housing clearance map, including the apex of this triangle, was even shaded as 'proposed slum clearance'.[2] The Grand Leeds Mosque stands near this apex now.

East of Woodsley Road several photographs focus on the 'Rosebanks', built across the steep hillside facing the river valley, on former pasture whose rent provided income for St John's Church in the city centre.[3] On the clearance map the 'Rosebanks' were gathered into the slightly less damning, but ominous, green boundary that enfolded Great Woodhouse as well: 'Houses to be dealt with under the Housing (Financial Provisions) Act 1958.'

As in the 'Lomonds', pre-redevelopment dereliction brought problems with squatters, and along came Councillor May Sexton again in 1969 to look for herself.[4] Some travellers had moved into Rosebank View by pulling boards down from empty houses. Fighting in the street, hurtling bottles and even personal threats and abuse frightened the neighbours, whose milk was disappearing from the doorsteps. Again Councillor Sexton expressed deep concern for the squatters as well as the residents: the reoccupied houses were overcrowded and had no sanitation. The council took action over their own houses but legally the responsibility for the others rested with their former owners (the Compulsory Purchase Order was still going through).[5]

Burley

With the building of new streets of houses, Little Woodhouse merged by degrees into neighbouring Burley, which has been included here partly because a visible boundary between the two is difficult to distinguish today. However, the original heart of Burley is on the far side of an impressive railway viaduct (see plate 02 for a map, and plates 11, 12 and 15) and some particularly interesting pictures were taken there with their own story to tell.

The Aire valley contains not just the river but the Leeds–Liverpool Canal, the railway lines to Ilkley and Harrogate and the A65 to Skipton (Kirkstall Road). The river's water power was a magnet for nineteenth-century mills and Kirkstall Road is still one of commercial premises up to and beyond the railway viaduct, where the line to Harrogate swings across the valley. Beyond the viaduct, however, streets of terraced houses surrounded Burley Church, behind a line of shops fronting Kirkstall Road, the nucleus of the Burley photographs.

On the 1834 map (on page 33) Burley was a hamlet away from the main road, on today's Burley Road. The building of St Matthias' in 1853–54 no doubt indicated an expanding population, boosted in due course by the redevelopment, in the 1860s to '80s, of the Earl of Cardigan's local estates, which ran from Kirkstall and Burley up to the very edge of Woodhouse Moor.[6] Thereafter terraced streets, some preserving the Cardigan family name 'Brudenell', joined Burley to Little Woodhouse and spread up to an area north-west of Woodhouse Moor now known as Hyde Park: hence 'Hyde Park Corner' on Woodhouse Lane, where Hyde Park Road meets the end of Woodhouse Street.

August 1968: Rosebank Road: The road runs from Woodsley Road along the crest of a steep hillside overlooking the Aire valley. The 'Rosebank' terraces were built along the slope below the road. There were houses on both sides of the road but today the right-hand side is completely open with a wide view over the valley (see plates 11 and 12).

November 1968: Rosebank Road. The old gas lamps feature prominently in these photographs. The man on the ladder at the far end of the road is reminiscent of the boy in RL Stevenson's poem about the lamplighter, hoping that one day 'Oh Learie I'll go round at night and light the lamps with you!' but this man may be just cleaning it – by 1968 it would probably have had a pilot light and timer to do Learie's work.

August 1996: The top of the steps in the picture opposite after redevelopment, with new houses below. The old railing and, just beyond that a curious piece of attached ironwork, still survived, replaced today by Millennium landscaping. As we peered into the distance, two small boys asked what we were doing. Colin showed them the 1968 photograph and one asked, 'So who took this?' When Colin said he did the lad looked at him and said, 'Cor, you must be ever so old!'

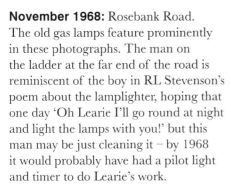

Opposite: **August 1968:** Rosebank Road. This long flight of steps linked the terraces below the road; they arrived in 1861 to enable the trustees of St John's, Leeds, to market their land below Rosebank Road for development. Ahead is the spire of St Matthias' Burley.

October 1969: Rosebank View. The washing is getting a good blow, but by December Councillor May Sexton was investigating reports of problems with squatters in the street.[7]

Opposite page:
Top: **November 1969:** Looking down from Rosebank Road into Rosebank View, the eye-watering steepness of the slope shows clearly in this view.

Bottom: **October 1969:** From Rosebank View the steps continued down to Rosebank Grove.

October 1969: Rosebank View. Nevertheless, in October the baby could still be put outside to get the fresh air and this little boy seems unconcerned about squatters.

October 1969: Hanover View. Like the 'Rosebanks', Hanover Avenue and View were above Burley Road but nearer the city centre. They were also part of May Sexton's ward and close to spacious old Hanover Square, where May and her husband Bert kept a bakery.

August 2013: Hill Top Road. All Hallows Church, as rebuilt in 1985 after its predecessor was destroyed by fire in 1970. The church is just off Hyde Park Road but its postal address is Burley.

August 1968: Kings Road off Hyde Park Road. The gable directly behind the lamp post is the west end of the old All Hallows, whose grounds are much higher than the road. The nearer gable was the former All Hallows Institute. Used as a school during the 1950s, it became a factory for Hartisca overalls and aprons. A former employee among the All Hallows worshippers told us that owner George Hart was a good employer, who still came in daily from Ripon at the age of 90. Residential accommodation on the site now bears the Hartisca name.

Kings Road today:
Part of the road survived redevelopment only as a footpath below the east end of the present All Hallows Church, supported on the same retaining wall as its predecessor.

April 2013: St Matthias', Burley, built in 1853–54 and paid for by John Smith of Burley House with the spire's cost met by William Beckett (1826–90) banker and Leeds politician.[8]

October 1969: Burley, from the railway embankment taking the line from Harrogate on to the long viaduct. Straight up St Matthias Place is the church tower, the larger houses to the right are on Burley Road. Today much of this area is covered by grass, with the new houses just around the church.

October 1969: Burley. A panorama looking towards Kirkstall; the shadow on the extreme left is the side of one of the former Kirkstall power station cooling towers. This is probably Amy Street with Minnie street to the right; St Matthias Street runs across at the end and the tree on the extreme right is in St Matthias' churchyard.

October 1969: A little further to the left, Minnie and Amy were kept company by Lilian Street and Place, backing onto the shops on Kirkstall Road (A65). Who were Minnie, Amy and Lilian? Were they the builder/speculator's wife and daughters? Kirkstall Power Station can be seen at the back.

October 1969: Minnie Street. This tiny shop at No. 11 is a good example of how what had started out as a house could become a very useful shop.

October 1969: Greenhow Avenue, Burley. West of St Matthias' Church were the 'Allertons' and Cardigan Lane, beyond which the 'Greenhows' ran parallel to Kirkstall Road. Their public inquiry didn't happen until March 1982. The surveyor was horrified to find a householder with two young children and no hot water, bath or hand basin, and with an external toilet 25m away. But the washing looks spotless and up the street comes the rag and bone man's horse and cart (see next chapter).

November 1968: Cardigan Mount. Cardigan Mount lay across Kirkstall Road opposite the 'Allertons' and Cardigan Lane. This shop seems to be based in the whole ground floor of a double-fronted house. Polony is an anglicised form of Bologna sausage.

Opposite: **May 1970:** St Johns Avenue. This large house stands on the corner with Moorland Road, along the west side of Woodhouse Moor, one of those built after 1855 to overlook it. A magnifying glass shows the name on the ladder as 'JW Brett & son decorators', based at 300 Kirkstall Road in the 1966 directory.

November 1969: Kirkstall Road. The terraces seen from the railway embankment backed onto these shops. RH Pullman the baker was at 308 Kirkstall Road in the 1961 and 1966 directories. In 1966 the chemist at No. 306 had been N Cagen, while CB Dalton's shop had been across Leeds at 97 Lidgett Lane. At No. 300, where the two ladies are chatting, was Mr Brett the decorator, whose name appears on the ladder in the last picture. All those shops have gone, replaced by open grassland between Kirkstall Road and the houses around St Matthias' (See colour plates 15 and 16).

March 1969: Walking the dog on Woodhouse Moor. Behind are the big houses built to overlook the park.

Chapter 4

Bringing the
Streets to Life

Up to this point the Woodhouse focus, especially in Chapter 2, has been on the preparations for redevelopment. But there was still more to life there than that, and the picture needs to be balanced by looking at the daily life that went on in these cosy houses: the community of family and neighbours, the doors that stood open to familiar passers-by and onto the street as a recreation area. If all your house windows look directly on to the same street, you surely identify very much with it and its communal life. It was lovingly recalled in 1980 by Rowland Lindup in his article for the *Dalesman*,[1] albeit with reference to an earlier decade.

Washing lines blowing cheerfully across the street are always fondly spoken of by older 'ex-patriots' of Leeds. In Rowland Lindup's day[2] it was a major operation: the water had to be boiled in a built-in 'set-pot' with a fire under it in the scullery, perhaps succeeded in a later decade by a gas-powered appliance called a 'copper'. The steaming washing, hauled out on a stick, had to go through a mangle or wringer and made heavy work. But satisfying on a fine day would be to see, as he described, 'the streets … festooned with clothes lines full of sheets, pillow slips, combs' (i.e. combinations) 'and articles of underwear'. He described the smell of washing powder in the air and clouds of steam billowing out of front doors, because in his day everyone tackled this on Mondays, so hanging it out could have been quite a sociable time. On a wet day, of course, it was a very different story. Colin's washing lines suggest that by 1967–70 the schedule wasn't so rigid. The washing machine and 'Ascot' water heaters had come on the scene, and although surveyors reported 'only a set-pot' for hot water in some places, another newcomer was the sociable launderette, glimpsed here on page 79.

Rowland Lindup called Friday 'spick and span' day, with housewives 'dusting, polishing, black leading, shaking the rugs, swilling the flags and donkey-stoning the doorstep'. The nostalgia shouldn't blind us to the heavy physical demands this work made on his mother and other housewives. By 1967–70 vacuum cleaners had taken over some of the work, but plate 09 shows the windowsills and doorstep still being washed. It was noted in Chapter 2 that coal-fired cooking ranges, glimpsed in Institution Street on page 49, had not gone completely out of use to make black-leading a thing of the past.

The quiet streets themselves were an informal social area and place for children to play. Rowland Lindup listed marbles, hopscotch, leapfrog, and hide and seek, as well as whip and top (see page 84) and skipping ropes (see page 83). Blank end-terrace gable walls were an open invitation to chalked cricket stumps and goal posts; the score from a game chalked on a wall can be glimpsed in the picture on page 19, taken in the 'Danubes'. The front doorstep was in frequent use as a seat and the corner shop provided chance encounters for neighbours to chat. All these things belonged to a way of life difficult to replicate from scratch in the new communities where residents were rehoused.

Outsiders did not really appreciate this: on one occasion it even reached a debate in the House of Lords, when Lady Denington claimed to have been 'horrified at what I saw going on' on a visit. 'Where,' she asked the bemused Lords 'does a woman in a back-to-back do her washing?' The equally bemused reaction back in Leeds was, 'Like most others we wash it in the kitchen and then hang it on a line!'[3]

Some photographs show the 'rag and bone man' with his horse and cart passing through collecting what might otherwise be dumped (see pages 70, 87, 88 and 101). During our on-site research, we fell into conversation with a young man on the corner opposite the scrap metal yard and had to explain to him what a rag and bone man was and how he represented some early recycling. Starting with rags for paper and shoddy, and bones for fertiliser, by 1970 he would be collecting metal and probably anything else that might prove useful somewhere to someone.

Opposite: **October 1969:** Ashfield Place. The 'Ashfields' lay between Cambridge and Oxford Roads. Across the end wall are the gables of the Perseverance Mills, which appear again in plate 23. It's a sunny October day and miniskirt and boots underline the date.

August 1968: Herbert Place, behind Oatland Lane. The washing hangs aloft. It was not unusual to park the baby outside for fresh air and probably someone had been enjoying the sun in that armchair, too. The door is open; they have perhaps just popped in for a brew.

May 1970: Booth Place, part of the 'North Wests', off Woodhouse Street. An inventive washing line. One wonders what the other end was attached to …

May 1970: Jubilee Terrace. The local launderette helped to take some of the labour out of wash day. A compulsory purchase order for at least part of Jubilee Road was made in 1971–72.[4]

July 1970: Jubilee Terrace. A sun-warmed doorstep was a favourite seat for children and animals alike. Ordnance Survey map evidence shows that the 'Jubilees', off Woodhouse Street, appeared after OS 1893, suggesting that they marked Queen Victoria's Diamond Jubilee in 1897.

May 1970: Grosvenor Hill. At the top of the steps up from Servia Hill these children are writing graffiti, presumably with chalk.

Opposite

Top: **April 1970:** Herbert Terrace, off Oatland Road. There are some nice details: the cleat with the washing line, the niche for a missing boot scraper and the open door. It's either been raining or the step and sills have been washed because you can see the dog's feet reflected in the pavement.

Bottom: **May 1970:** Servia Avenue. The gradient suggests the upper part of the street, between Servia Road and Servia Hill. A hot bath in front of the fire would be cosy in the winter time but found no favour with the 1957 Act's standards.

April 1970: Danube Terrace, Leeds 12. Out of our area but close to Wortley where Rowland Lindup grew up in the 1920s or '30s. Children play in the street, where the skipping ropes are out.

April 1972: Eldon Place, above St Mark's. A little girl is whipping a top, as children were probably doing in those streets in Victorian times. It is worth noting, however, that in the 1970s a new interest in past customs, perhaps a reaction against 1960s modernism, brought traditional wooden toys to the fore again. They were sometimes a woodworker's sideline for sale at craft fairs. A whipped top needed practice to make it work!

May 1970: Duxbury Place. Dogs roaming in and out of doors and children outside, watchful neighbours ready to help where needed. As the shutter clicked one little lad appears to have knocked the other flying but someone is arriving through the door, while a dog is coming to investigate too! Several people gather at the other end of the street where the washing is blowing.

August 1968: Claypit Street. Two lads relax on the doorstep (foreground) and a conversation takes place at the far end with not only a washing line but a clothes airer standing outside as well.

May 1970: Woodhouse Street. The loaded rag and bone cart passes a piece of open ground backing on to the big houses off Cliff Road. Woodhouse Street would have taken the dealer to Meanwood Road, where he would have come out near the scrap metal business.

Opposite: **October 1969:** Oatland Lane. Encountering a friend at the corner shop: a welcome chance to chat for a housewife at home while the family were at school or work. Trade directories show that WBA at No. 159 was William Baden Ackroyd.

May 1970: Haslewood Close, Leeds 9. Among later houses the rag and bone cart has stopped for lunch, and the horse is enjoying his nosebag and attention from the children.

Chapter 5

Shops, Shopping and Economic Changes

Colin has always liked taking pictures of shops. One of the fascinating things about many shop pictures is the glimpse of advertisements, goods and sometimes what they cost, for example on page 72 and colour plate 19. The corner shop was an especially important feature of back-to-back communities.

When tentative second thoughts about the effects of wholesale clearances on townscape character and established communities were starting to be heard, The *Yorkshire Evening Post* joined in the discussion. It pointed out that the closely knit terraces 'with their cobbled streets, corner shops, Co-op, chapel, pub and free library' combined to 'make up an environment that has dignity and an austere kind of charm'. Of the corner shops, it went on to say, 'The shop rents are reasonable and the traders are able to lend a willing ear, give advice and credit, and make the hundred and one little contributions to the community that spanking new supermarkets can never make.'[1]

The corner shop has already been flagged up as a place where friends could be encountered and news exchanged. In 1967 John Waddington-Feather wrote euphorically of the city's Herculean rehousing project, emphasising the 'spacious surroundings' enjoyed by the houses in the new estates. As in the Quarry Hill 'vision' in 1935, he claimed that the Lincoln Green development would have its own shopping centre, 'like most other new estates'.[2] Even if they did, sometimes a higher rent for the shop raised the prices of the goods. Sadly time has shown that small corner shops have found survival difficult today, even where redevelopment has not been a factor. The rise of the supermarket ushered in a serious competitor.

These pictures also show a trade in second-hand furniture, perhaps sometimes on a short-term let in vacated shops whose days were numbered. Was there a trade boost as people began moving house in large numbers, some to a flat smaller than their old home? A letter to the *Evening Post* in 1973 regretted the impending loss of the attic and the cellar: 'Where can Mum store that old chair that needs mending, or the old suite that the bin-men won't take away, or the old cupboard that might come in handy some day? In our attic we can store anything we may need or that may come in useful some day.' The writer also had an intriguing use for the cellar: 'Where does father have room for his hobby in a council house? In our old back-to-back he can play quite happily in the cellar without making a mess for Mum to clear up.'[3]

Included here also is a group of larger shops much closer to the city in North Street, the urban continuation of Meanwood Road (see plate 01). These were 'almost city' shops but local enough to be accessible on foot for some residents of Woodhouse and its neighbour Sheepscar, or a short bus ride away,[4] and not far from Kirkgate market. Among their later economic problems would be the loss of regular customers who had moved away, whose old homes for a crucial period left only an empty space. These photographs suggest a period of unmistakeable decline: some businesses had themselves moved away, perhaps to a better position; commercial redevelopment has left none of them standing now.

Opposite: **August 1968:** Hawkins Street. This little shop was an off-licence but we haven't been able to trace the licensee, CM Vasey. The street was next to Kenealy Street, and part of the little group of terraces off Oatland Lane that included Livinia Street and Duxbury Place.

May 1970: Cambridge Road. We can't be sure exactly where this off-licence was as we couldn't trace the licensee in any directories. But this rather ornate frontage is reminiscent of a small pub; in the 1947 Kelly's Directory Mrs Carrie Hurst was a beer retailer between Claro Avenue and Claro Place at 21 Cambridge Road. Next came a grocer, then Claro Terrace and then the Church of the Holy Name, at the Woodhouse Street fork with Servia Road.

Clockwise from top left:

May 1970: Cambridge Road. The local chippie on the corner with Vaughan Street. Mr Lindup, remembering his Wortley childhood, recalled Friday as 'tuppeny and pennyworth day', with the choice of a tail or a middle.[5] The price had increased greatly by 1970!

May 1970: 92 St Mark's Road. A tiny shop on the corner of (upper) St Mark's Road and Bagby Street. John Hastings had a fruit shop here in 1932 and Gilbert Haig Gath, shopkeeper, was there in 1947. Thereafter No. 92 disappears: the even numbers in the directories end at 90. It may then have been a shop only with no one living on the premises.

May 1973: The corner of Blackman Lane with Well Close Terrace. Business looks brisk; the lights are on and the lads outside look as if they're ready for a good night out, suggesting that this was taken in the early evening. VP Wine was produced by Vine Products of Kingston upon Thames.

Opposite and above: **July 1970:** St Mark's Road. The position of the 'Kandy Kabin' at No. 98, couldn't be checked by name, but Nos 98 and 100 were on the north side of (upper) St Mark's Road, on either corner of 'Back Eldon Street'. In 1947 Mrs Annie Copley was a shopkeeper at 98, only a few doors up from the little shop at No. 92.

June 1970: Alexandra Road. Alexandra Road is off Hyde Park Road near the Hyde Park Road–Woodsley Road triangle apex. Sadly this butcher's shop with the eye-catching bull's head keystone has gone.

April 1970: Domestic Terrace, Leeds 11. The same butcher had another shop here; he was clearly proud of his slogan above the door! No sign of this shop remains either and a lady we spoke to in Domestic Street recalled several local butchers but did not recognise this one.

(Plate 01) Map of 'Great Woodhouse' in the 1960s, including Little London, as covered by this book. Based on a contemporary street atlas with our boundary roads in orange and other important roads in yellow. Please note: Camp Road on the map = Oatland Lane (see Chapter 2). Similarly New Camp Road = Servia Hill.

Some names were omitted by the mapmakers for lack of space: where relevant we refer them to a nearby street name printed on the map.

(Plate 02) Map showing Little Woodhouse and Burley in the 1960s. They are not named on the map but roads important to placing the photographs have been shaded yellow, also St Matthias' Church, Burley, and All Hallows off Hyde Park Road.

(Plate 03) **February 1968:** Woodhouse Lane: The University clock tower at night.

(Plate 04) **February 1969:** Woodhouse Moor under snow. Former pasture between Woodhouse and Little Woodhouse, acquired by the city as a park in 1855.

(Plate 05) **December 1967:** Raglan Road, looking down from Woodhouse Moor. Terraced streets cluster around the tower of Quarry Mount School. The sharp angle of Cathcart Street and Raglan Road and the warmly glowing old gas lamp were typical area features. The group of post-war prefabs replaced a collection of irregular little courts cleared in the 1930s.

(Plate 06) **October 1967:** Institution Street. The building with white quoins on the right is the Temperance Hall Mechanics Institute, which gave the street its name. Costing £900, it was built in 1851 as an alternative social centre to the pubs.[1] Unlike the rest of the street, the 'institute' is still standing and in use as a community church.

1. For the background to this see 'George Lucas and the Leeds Temperance Movement' posted by Leeds Libraries, 14 December 2017, on www.secretlibraryleeds.net

Clockwise from above:
(Plate 07) **November 1967:** Ashworth
Street. This cul-de-sac ran down
from St Mark's Road to end behind
Stockdale Terrace on Institution Street.

(Plate 08) **January 1968:** Churchfield
Terrace, a cul-de-sac above Institution
Street. Washing the doorstep (and the
windowsills) was an important part of
keeping the home shipshape.

(Plate 09) **March 1968:** at the top of
Institution Street. The last picture on
the roll of film: it could have meant
half a picture or none at all when
Kodak returned the slides. The result
was this square frame. Meanwhile,
returning later to repeat the picture,
Colin found that the entire site had
been cleared. It shows how quickly the
streetscape could change for ever.

(Plate 10) **December 1967:** Well Close Road. A wintry afternoon view showing the long slope, down an old field boundary, to the Meanwood Beck valley. The houses in the background are probably on Savile Drive, off Chapeltown Road (the A61 to Harrogate).

(Plate 11) **October 1967:** The Aire valley from Abyssinia Place. The Kirkstall railway viaduct crosses the centre of the picture; the Kirkstall power station behind it has now gone along with the clustered mill chimneys in the valley.

(Plate 12) **June 2014:** The same view from Rosebank Road. The railway viaduct helps comparison with the 1967 picture from Abyssinia Place.

Clockwise from top left:

(Plate 13) **October 1967:** Milford Place, taken from the bridge over the River Aire. Across Kirkstall Road is St Matthias' Church, Burley. All the foreground buildings have now been replaced by light commercial units and the shops on Kirkstall Road, looked at in detail in Chapter 3, have gone.

(Plate 14) **October 1967:** Corner shop on Kings Road, between Burley and Little Woodhouse. All these houses have gone, although there is still a Hartwell Road. See also photos 059 and 060.

(Plate 15) **November 2014:** The site of the Kirkstall Road shops today. The row ran behind today's bus shelter up to the former Rising Sun in the centre of the picture, derelict for several years at time of writing, with the railway viaduct beyond.

2. Wrathmell, 2005, p.194.

(Plate 16) **October 1967:** The partly cleared apex of the Woodsley Road/Hyde Park Road triangle point in Little Woodhouse. The Leeds Grand Mosque stands there now. The paved area in the foreground had been Victoria Mount. Ahead Armley Church crowns the skyline across the industrialised Aire valley.

(Plate 17) **March 1968**: Kelsall Road, between Little Woodhouse and Burley. The 'Kelsalls' were built in 1886 over the grounds of a big house called Burley Lodge and take their name from its last occupant: William Kelsall, Mayor of Leeds in 1859. These lucky terraces were improved in the 1960s and enjoyed further upgrading measures between 1995 and 2002.[2] Above the roofs is the tower of All Hallows Church, seen before the 1970 fire referred to in Chapter 3.

Clockwise from top: (Plate 18) **October 1967:** Greenhow Terrace, Burley. 'Corner shops' were often built in pairs, back-to-back across the end of two terraces. Between them these two could probably have supplied anything. Mr Robinson's was not just a provisions shop: close inspection of the white lettering shows he could even see you right for plumbing, electrical and roof repairs. (Plate 19) **April 2019:** Shops on Woodsley Road, Little Woodhouse. Changes since the 1968 picture on page 97 (Chapter 5) reflect today's lifestyle: the chemist's neighbour is now Best Cuts (hairdresser) and the former Post Office has become Computer Corner. The mailbox is still just visible outside, but the post office has moved downhill to Londis on the corner of Westfield Road. The Big T Cafe has become the Double Dragon takeaway. (Plate 20) **November 1976:** Pat's grocery shop on Meanwood Road. Sadly, Pat's shop has defied all our attempts to find out exactly where it was. This end terrace just might be the end of Ormonde Place, where the end shop was at one time a grocer's but some frontage details make this a little doubtful. As a record of 1970s prices her shop window is fascinating.

(Plate 21) **April 2023:** Woodhouse Street. The foodstore on the corner of Midgley Terrace, with new 'Holborns' houses behind.

(Plate 22) **July 1971:** Servia Hill. The angled junction of Servia Hill (leading to St Marks Road) with Servia Road running off the picture to the left. The sun falls on the lamp post at the other sharp fork at the bottom of Grosvenor Hill.

(Plate 23) **January 1973:** A young couple waiting for a bus on Servia Road. The upper road is Servia Hill, but the photographer is looking down from Grosvenor Hill. Ashfield Terrace and Place in the background mark the line of Cambridge Road but the Cambridge Road and Oxford Road terraces have gone. At the back are the Perseverance Mills with the name 'Peter Laycock Ltd, woollen manufacturer'. Converted to student accommodation, it has kept the name 'Perseverance Mill'.

(Plate 24) **November 1976:** Looking down Woodhouse Street. Holborn Tower helps show how everything up to Craven Road has been flattened. New 'Elthams' will arise here named after a former set of terraces. In front of the tower stand the new 'Holborns'. In the background the white Marquis of Lorne pub stands out. The tallest chimney of the three is Bray's Bagby Works chimney on Grosvenor Hill.

(Plate 25) **May 1978:** at the bottom of Blackman Lane, below All Souls' church. The man crossing the carpet of grass and bricks is perhaps contemplating the changes. Much of this area, probably including the upper parts of the Livinia to Hawkins group of streets, has been left open and grassed.

(Plate 26) **June 2014:** Looking up today's Hawkins Drive towards that green area and All Souls Blackman Lane. Livinia Grove and Duxbury Rise lie away to the right of Hawkins Drive, keeping the old names alive.

(Plate 27) **May 2016:** Oatland Lane. The flight of steps down from Grosvenor Hill, seen in Chapter 2 (page 40), has survived. They now lead down a green bank to the Oatland Lane and Woodhouse Street bus route from the city.

(Plate 28) **April 2023:** Looking down Woodhouse Street, towards the Charing Cross shopping centre and 'Johnny Benn's' flats, the former Marquis of Lorne (see page 120): A near equivalent to plate 24 taken during redevelopment in 1976.

(Plate 29) **April 2019:** Quarry Mount School. This fine old school building's lofty clock tower, on rising ground, is a landmark in this part of Woodhouse. It is a Grade 2 listed building, built in 1885. The name 'A Dougill Leeds' is cast on every main post of its impressive railings. His firm appears in directories around 1900 as an engineer, millwright – and motor car manufacturer!

(Plate 30) **April 2013:** Looking down Glossop Street from below Quarry Mount School, whose railings are on the left. Around it the back-to-back terraces of Thomas Street, Christopher Road, the 'Beulahs', Quarry Place and Quarry Street, Providence Road and Avenue were reprieved from impending redevelopment in 1978.

October 1969: Woodsley Road. These shops are still there opposite the Hyde Park Road fork. The bay window beyond the wall has been rebuilt since as a shop (chemist) and all the shop fronts have been remodelled. The 1969 prices on the board outside the Big T cafe are interesting. Plate 20 is a recent picture of the row.

May 1970: Westfield Crescent. The Westfields were in the angle of Woodsley Road and Burley Road. On the corner of Burley Road, J Townsend seems to be selling chiefly china and earthenware and is hoping we'll venture over the threshold. It still forms the end of a row of Burley Road shops with two storeys of living accommodation above.

October 1969: Cambridge Road. Back in Woodhouse these may be signs of the times: temporary lets selling second hand goods in shops which have closed. Frequent house moves were taking place because of the clearances. Lack of storage space in the new flats may well have led to downsizing house contents.

Opposite: **April 2019:** The same shop is now a snack bar but above it is this old painted sign – to the astonishment of the proprietor, who had wondered what we were looking at. 'Brown's' shop seems to have had a higher profile than Mr Townsend's 1970 emporium but efforts to trace him have not proved fruitful! No. 90 was a milliner's shop in 1910 and in the 1930s and later was a chemist. None bore the name Brown: perhaps at one time this shop traded under its own name but the enterprising 'Mr Brown' owned it!

1969: Oatland Lane: Shops opposite the bottom of Grosvenor Hill on the cusp of change. The chemist Kenneth R Rutter MPS, at No. 114 Oatland Lane in the 1968 telephone directory, would be gone by 1973. Mr Ali at 113 has already moved on; the new trader hasn't felt a change of sign worth doing.

Opposite page:

Top: **September 1968:** Roundhay Road. Outside our area but included for the furniture Andy was selling. The little table with twisted legs may belong with a fashion for 'Jacobean' styles *c.*1890–1930: the raised back of the white table shows it may be a bedroom washstand. The bureau-cum-display cabinet could be 1930s or as late as 1950. Andy was probably using the empty grocer's next door for storage.

Bottom: **April 1979:** Meanwood Road. The rag and bone man isn't running a shop but he is carrying something relevant that someone feels they no longer need. A zinc bath, if not full size, is perched on the cart between his two passengers. E Ross is now Ross Metal Recycling and still in the same place, next but one to the Primrose pub (see page 130) at the bottom of Buslingthorpe Lane.

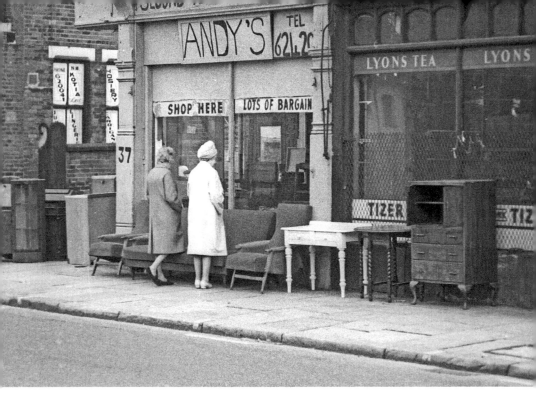

May 1970: Ormonde Place, Meanwood Road. Despite its run-down appearance this tall terrace has survived. At the nearer end was Sackville Street post office. Two shops show links with the cloth trade: to left of the post office was R Thompson gents tailor 'own materials made up', and next but one had been Henry or Harry Neal 'Fashion Wear'. John Parker's name is clear but what he was selling isn't! By 2019 Ormonde Place had been spruced up and sadly all but one of those distinctive chimneys had gone.

May 1970: Ormonde Place, showing a closer view of the post office's window. The poster on the left is difficult to see but reads 'Fishing tragedies at sea … What then?' At the General Election on Thursday, 7 May 1970 Councillor May Sexton was hoping to become MP for South East Leeds but lost out to Labour. She claimed that 'since the last General Election 4,000 electors have moved from the constituency due to slum clearance'. A keen eye can still see faint vertical white lines on the walls of Ormonde Place marking where these poster boards once were.

November 1972: North Street. The sequence of odd numbers suggests that these shops were on the west side of this major route into the city. The closure of John Mee Woollen Merchants & Manufacturers, at 83 North St in 1966, does not appear recent. Gerald Garner China & Glass, just visible extreme right, was at No. 87 in 1972 but not in 1973, and the window display doesn't look like china! TR Electrics at No. 85 had been L & DI Furniss Shop Displays in 1966.

May 1970: North Street. Signs of decline: S & J Mathers Ltd, Toys, Prams, Drapers, at No. 149 in 1969, state on their sale sign that 'This business will shortly be transferred', probably to their other premises in Leeds 8 and 9. Barrett & Firestone Ltd, Ladies Tailors had been next door in 1966. No. 151 on the right was empty from 1955 through to 1966 but someone had had at least a temporary let more recently.

April 1970: North Street. The two ladies chatting outside TR Electrics, one with a shopping bag, are a reminder that North Street was not far from Sheepscar and Woodhouse, and close to the Briggate shops and Kirkgate Market. These shops had probably picked up much passing trade.

May 1970: North Street. A second-hand goods dealer and some long-term history. Shermans Sports outfitters were at No. 155 in 1966, with William Turton (Leeds Ltd) Forage Merchant here at No. 153. 'William Turton hay & straw dealer' was already there in 1894 and was perhaps the original proprietor of these late Victorian commercial premises. Storage of such materials might explain the ventilated panels at the top of the huge doors.

Chapter 6

The Changing Landscape in the 1970s

At the end of Chapter 2, the Woodhouse redevelopment plans were paused at the point where individual properties were becoming empty and then derelict, boarded up until the whole street could be demolished for rebuilding. The story told by the pictures moves on now into the transformation of residential Woodhouse into what we see today. In some ways it is a more positive story because the problems of vandalism and squatters in derelict houses would cease in any given area when there was no house to squat in, however forlorn the vacant space appeared. The die was cast, the buildings had gone and, literally, the only way was up.

On the other hand, it was the final goodbye to people's homes, lovingly maintained to the point of departure by their occupants, whose regrets surface sometimes in the surveyors' reports and at public inquiries. Many of the houses were rented but some were privately owned by the householders. At the Livinia Street public inquiry in 1969, an elderly resident said that her house in the street was all she owned and she had expected to spend the rest of her days there. She hoped that, if it really had to go, she would be compensated adequately.[1] Livinia Street was part of the 'Oatland Lane/ Bristol Road' clearance area, which included the group of streets seen in earlier chapters that were linked by Hawkins Place, from Kenealy Street to the 'Lomonds'. In summer 1970, a year after the Inquiry, we see Livinia Street being cleared.

Opposite: **May 1970:** North Street. What could be nicer than sitting in the sun when you haven't a customer? Sadly we couldn't find a North Street Gents hairdresser in the directories but this surely wasn't a newly established shop.

The photographs mark the progress of rebuilding in areas that, said Professor Beresford with a characteristic turn of phrase, 'await the phoenix that the City Engineer will some day raise from their ashes and rubble'.[2] That included the expanse of 'Little London', bordering Oatland Lane and already empty, across which the Claypit Lane dual carriageway was later taken. We see two 'Oatland' blocks of flats being built in 1970 and finished 'Oatland' houses standing there by May 1973. A bleak snowy view in January 1973 (plate 23) shows much of Servia Road completely cleared, along with Cambridge and Oxford Roads; the 'Herberts' behind Oatland Lane must soon have followed suit, but we see washing still hanging out there early in 1973 and milk was still being delivered in November 1972 (page 112).

By 1975 new houses are seen standing where Duxbury Place and 'The Lomonds' had been at the foot of Grosvenor Hill, with new houses called 'Servia Drive' rising along the old line of Servia Road. Plate 24 shows lower Woodhouse Street in November 1976 reduced to bare ground, below the newly built 'Holborns' at the foot of Holborn Tower.

November 1972:
Wintoun Street, off
North Street. The stretch
of land in Little London,
bordering Oatland
Lane and cleared by
the mid 1960s, would
have been the obvious
place to begin rebuilding
Woodhouse, providing
much-needed new
accommodation. The
Lovell Park tower blocks
were first to arrive.

1970 May: Off Oatland
Lane, Little London.
The three Lovell Park
blocks appear in the
background beyond the
bridge over the dual
carriageway. Oatland
Court, close to the road,
and Oatland Towers, in
the foreground, are seen
under construction.

1970 May: A closer view of Oatland Court under construction.

November 1972: Off Oatland Lane looking towards the 'Herberts'. These new houses are also being built on that cleared land, close to where General Wade had camped in 1745. They may be today's Oatland Close. In the background is Bray's factory chimney on Grosvenor Hill.

May 1970: Herbert Place, behind Oatland Lane. The 'Herberts', near the junction with Grosvenor Hill, were gradually being emptied by 1970. Occasionally Colin ventured into an abandoned house if it was accessible and this picture looks out from empty No. 3 Herbert Place.

November 1972: 'No. 3' in one of the 'Herberts'. Not Herbert Place, because we know from the previous picture that No. 3 was derelict in 1970. This must be Herbert Street or Terrace.

Early in 1973: Herbert Place. Someone's washing still flutters bravely in the breeze but perhaps not for much longer. The other side of the new houses under construction can be seen across Oatland Road. But where on earth did that tree trunk come from?

May 1973: Some of the new houses on Oatland Green have been completed. Across the new primary school and Oatland Lane is a glimpse of All Souls Blackman Lane.

May 1970: Kenealy Street. A contrast between old and new across Oatland Lane: the chimneys of Kenealy Street are seen against the Carlton Croft tower block just behind. Smoke rises from a chimney but the nearest window is boarded up.

May 1970: Livinia Street[3] just before demolition. Like Hawkins Street, Livinia Street ran down across Hawkins Place to Oatland Lane, near the junction with Grosvenor Hill. On the right, below the sheet, Duxbury Place comes in at an angle. Everything looks normal, but there are ominously boarded windows on the right (see also page 118).

Opposite: **April 1970:** Hawkins Street. This is Kenealy Street's neighbour: a young lad strolls casually down towards Oatland Lane.

Spring 1973: Waiting for the bus down on Servia Road, on the far side of 'the Herberts'. These derelict houses were part of the 'Servias', probably the last ones to go.

Summer 1970: Livinia Street: Since May 1970, everything up to Hawkins Place has gone. On a more cheerful note, the names Duxbury, Hawkins and Livinia have been perpetuated in the later on-site developments, below All Souls Blackman Lane, whose tower can be seen in the background. (see plate 26).

February 1975: The bottom of Grosvenor Hill. This is the old Grosvenor Hill 'point' after demolition. The road now runs past it straight up Servia Hill to St Mark's Road. The new houses of Servia Drive stand on the old course of Servia Road, which was diverted to just beyond the Wimpey sign. It now turns right down to Cambridge Road and Woodhouse Street, taking the bus route with it.

February 1975: The lower end of Grosvenor Hill: The VP Wine advertisement marks the end of Grosvenor Avenue, with the ends of Grosvenor Street and Blackman Lane behind. These new houses are on the site of 'the Lomonds' and Duxbury Place; today they front an abbreviated Grosvenor Hill, with a green slope down to Oatland Lane.

April 2023: Woodhouse Street and Johnny Benn's: Originally known as the Marquis of Lorne, this old pub survived the surrounding redevelopment, to be known latterly as 'The Beer Exchange', but closed in 2007. Johnny Benn was a popular landlord and his name – and most of the frontage – has survived conversion since into flats.[4]

April 2019: Midgley Terrace, Woodhouse Street: Today's local shops are in Woodhouse Street and the little Charing Cross shopping centre next to Johnny Benn's. The shop in this picture is part of the 1930s development on the site of Midgley Square.

Chapter 7

The 'Woodhouse (Rider Road) Clearance Area' and a Reprieve for Some Householders

The area between Woodhouse Street and Woodhouse Ridge has been left until last because it has a particular place in the redevelopment story of Woodhouse, and it was the last part of the old core area to receive attention. By the date that happened however, in the late 1970s, we had no permanent connections in Leeds: the chapter has therefore been compiled with photographs taken earlier than the events described and more recent pictures.

By the mid 1970s new thoughts were being aired. It was a decade wherein there was an increasing respect for post-medieval archaeology, industrial archaeology and, inevitably, the importance of retaining the tangible remains associated with both. Importantly, they were branches of history where active participation did not need academic qualifications, because new local societies were springing up needing volunteers to record this and that and even, as railway and steam engine enthusiasts joined in, to bring it back to life.[1] A new popular awareness of history was a logical outcome – and a new realisation that it didn't stop at some point in the distant past or even yesterday: even the present is tomorrow's history.

The post-war to 1960s 'out with the old, in with the new' vision was being challenged by a new awareness of 'local identity' and its characteristics. In Leeds a new focus fell on the older housing stock's contribution to local topographical character. The penny had finally dropped that the old terraced streets represented more than bricks and mortar, even while the same bricks and mortar were being systematically flattened. Some of the less tangible hallmarks of street life on which Chapter 4 is based were being viewed more seriously. As early as 1973 the *Yorkshire Evening Post* had pointed to: the 'cobbled streets, corner shops, co-op, chapel, pub and "free library"'[2] as pieces of a whole greater than the sum of its parts.

It would be wrong to say that all back-to-back occupiers themselves were reluctant to move. When the *Yorkshire Evening Post* commiserated with the Woodhouse residents' fight to save at least some of their old homes, householders elsewhere in Richmond Hill and East Park were quick to respond that they were very pleased that their own houses were coming down and moving day couldn't come soon enough![3]

The residents of the 'Woodhouse (Rider Road) Clearance Area', from Woodhouse Street up past Rider Road itself to Melville Place on the crest of Woodhouse Ridge, thought very differently. Their retention in the Housing Renewal Programme had been confirmed in 1972, divided into three areas for attention over 1977–81.[4] The residents set up 'The Woodhouse Housing Action Group' and in May 1976 issued their own report. It opposed wholesale clearance and, while accepting that some local properties were probably unfit for long-term occupation, pleaded for gradual renewal of the remainder. In November the Leeds Housing Services Committee, after lengthy discussion, decided upon a feasibility study of the whole of the area concerned. A study group was set up to prepare their own report as the basis for a public participation exercise. Three meetings took place in July 1978 between the study group, the ward councillors and the residents. A further meeting in October included the Woodhouse Community Association, described as 'a combination of various bodies opposed to a policy of clearance'. A major champion of the residents throughout was the Rev. Robert Simpson, vicar of St Mark's.

In December 1978 the Housing Services Committee issued its final report, including an interesting thumbnail picture summing up the variety among the overall householders: 'Within a single block of property … (there may be) a widowed pensioner living next door to a dwelling occupied as a bed-sitter by three to four students, the next door again (*sic*) there may be a recently married couple in their first home.' The final verdict, however, brought good news for some but not for all. In addition to the 1957 Act's standards for habitable dwellings, certain features of the local Woodhouse topography re-emerged, long forgotten perhaps but commemorated in the name of Quarry Mount School: the former extensive quarries in the hillside above it. On the 1850 Ordnance Survey they form a swathe across the back of the Ridge as 'Woodhouse Quarries (Sandstone)'. OS 1893 shows four distinct 'Old Quarries' as craters, well above the school. By the 1906 edition, Melville Place along the top of the Ridge, Rider Road, the 'Gantons' and the 'Hawes' stood right on top of them. The 1978 findings suggest that back-filling allowed insufficient time for the ground to settle before house-building followed.

The effects of instability featured strongly in the individual property surveys that followed the 1978 report and certainly the 'Gantons' and 'Hawes' were not reprieved by any second thoughts over wholesale redevelopment. Their demolition zone included one side of neighbouring Glossop View, where a resident objected strongly in 1980, 'I understand that the back to backs in the Gantons with no hot water, no inside toilets and damp want to come down but not ours', which was a 'through' house with a bathroom.[5] Sadly it may just have been on the wrong side of the road, because the 'even numbers' of Glossop View still stand, facing a pleasant green area which was once the 'Hawes'.

Of the Rider Road Clearance Area's three components, the fate of Areas 1 (The 'Gantons') and 2 (The 'Hawes', Golcar Street and Glossop Terrace) remained unchanged. Immediate clearance of areas 1 and 2 was stipulated 'because there is a lot of instability as well as poor condition'. But in 'Woodhouse area 3', immediately around and below the school, there was good news for the residents. Some of the streets around Quarry Mount School were being recommended for a cost assessment 'to determine the financial viability of rehabilitation'.

Nevertheless, a public inquiry took place in July 1980, at which the preservation case was argued by the Rev. Robert Simpson and the residents, along with the Leeds Civic Trust. The inspector, however, supported the Housing Services Committee's decision with regard to Areas 1 and 2, and in December 1980 the Secretary of State confirmed his agreement with the inspector's findings. Indeed, while it might have been valid to claim that the staircases in areas 1 and 2 (which were stated to be 'worn,' 'dark', 'steep and winding' and sometimes innocent of handrails, plus the usually cited lack of through ventilation) may well have been no more irremediable than those down in Area 3, the instability factor was a 'given' impossible to ignore. Demolition ensued for the 'Gantons', 'Hawes' and Golcar Street, along with Hartley Crescent and Avenue and Melville Place up on the Ridge, and for Elm Street and Johnston Street below, with parts of Rider Road and Glossop View.[6]

The surveyors' remarks below have been taken from the Ganton View surveys as a random sample of those taken in Areas 1 and 2. Some criticisms of individual properties seem quite petty now, relating to the easily remedied condition of fittings like cookers and sinks; one was even 'structurally sound but dirty due to 2 kids, 1 dog and 1 cat'. It even had 'bathroom, dormer', suggesting that the landlord had taken advantage of the installation grant to extend the property's life for up to fifteen years. But elsewhere in the street there was much sympathy from the surveyors: next door to the above a pensioner had lived in the house for forty-five years and next door again was a house 'very well looked after internally by tenants'. Elsewhere elderly residents for sixty years had 'washing accommodation in kitchen. Bath in kitchen', perhaps under a big table top[7] but 'no hot water in house. Pot enamel sink. Gas. Outside toilet. Not re-wired …' but nevertheless 'house very well kept by tenants'.[8]

Above the 'Gantons', was Melville Place, backing onto Woodhouse Ridge. Not all the houses along the Ridge were demolished: those that were bordered also the sloping end of Melville Place down towards Meanwood Road. Not back-to-back and unlikely therefore to have been troubled by lack of through ventilation, they too may have shown signs of subsidence, especially as, like the 'Hawes', their site was left as grass.

Below the 'Gantons' lay Johnston Street, the southern boundary of this clearance area. Johnston Street has been completely rebuilt, except where two preserved 'Beulahs' and lower Elm Street adjoin it, and the new houses back onto the open green. Parts of it were under the redevelopment microscope as early as 1960–61; twenty-six houses there had only one room downstairs plus bedroom and six more still had a cellar kitchen.[9] Both the street name and the old Chemic Tavern that stands at its junction with Woodhouse Street recall the former Johnston's Woodhouse Chemical Works, which bordered the street in the 1890s.[10] It supplied several Woodhouse dye works, some of which lay on Meanwood Road to benefit from the soft water of Meanwood Beck.

In Area 3, however, several streets of back-to-back terraces escaped further threat and survive today: Christopher Road, Thomas Street and Quarry Place and Street around the school, and Glossop Street and the 'Beulahs' between there and Johnston Street, plus two 'Providences' on the far side of the school (plate 30). The wave of conservationist thinking was beginning to militate against back-to-backs being considered *ipso facto* impossible to ventilate adequately, with the support of national organisations such as SAVE Britain's Heritage.[11] In 1981 the northern secretary of SAVE commented, 'It is difficult to see why Leeds City Council condemns housing without a back door yet re-houses people in blocks of flats which open only onto a corridor.'[12] To be fair, the design of the flats usually enabled good ventilation via the arrangement of windows.

Even by February 1977 the *Yorkshire Evening Post* had felt able to announce with a picturesque turn of phrase that, 'Many of the dilapidated old houses of Leeds are being saved from the bulldozers that once roamed the city streets devastating whole areas.'[13] The policy of comprehensive redevelopment was finally abandoned in 1984, with the result that whole areas of terraces have survived in Leeds to tell the tale: modernised, well maintained and recognised as a vital characteristic of the city's landscape and part of its heritage.[14]

In December 1985, the *Weekend Post* recorded some interesting statistics. In March 1943 there had been 74,720 back-to-back houses standing in Leeds, of which almost 33,500 had been built before 1872. These last may perhaps have included some of the long unbroken terraces that preceded the blocks of eight; they had been an immediate demolition target in the wake of the 1930 act. In 1973 30,000 of the houses had survived the mass redevelopment; by December 1985 the number had dropped to 19,000,[15] roughly the figure still variously cited now on the internet.

1972: Upper St Mark's Road from the corner of Bagby Terrace. We did not really encounter evidence of active organised protest against the redevelopment before the formation of the Woodhouse Housing Action Group in 1976, but here someone has made their feelings very clear to the council! A Bagby Fields Clearance Area public inquiry had certainly taken place in July 1971.[16] The key to making the Housing Services Committee take notice was good organisation and publicity: the Woodhouse Housing Action Group, fighting for the threatened streets between Woodhouse Street and Woodhouse Ridge, seem to have managed this very well.

October 1967: Pennington Street. This picture shows the gradient of the hillside beside Quarry Mount School, from Woodhouse Ridge down to Woodhouse Street. The rear school building in the foreground behind the railed playground no longer stands, although traces of its entrance gate can still be spotted in the boundary wall.

OFF LICENSE
SHOP
Dutton's
ALES
OBJ

GANTON MOUNT

GANTON PLACE

July 1968: Elm Street. Looking uphill to the roofs of Rider Road. On the right are the ends of Ganton Mount and Ganton Place. These are streets built between 1893 and 1906 over the old quarries.

May 1970: Melville Place. The road still runs along the crest of Woodhouse Ridge, dropping down towards Meanwood Road. These houses have gone and the space left empty. Down below the Primrose pub on Meanwood Road is still there but no longer visible from Melville Place. Johnston Street runs off to the right.

Opposite page:

Top: **November 1976:** Ganton View. Despite their spruce exterior appearance the 'Gantons' were doomed by instability. The detection of structural problems meant no hope of the reprieve granted to streets lower down below the old quarry line.

Bottom: **November 1976:** Looking across Melville Place to Rider Road from the steps down onto Woodhouse Ridge. The Gantons bent round to the right behind Rider Road. All these houses were demolished on the grounds of potential instability.

November 2013: Meanwood Road. A view of the Primrose pub today and its surroundings including the remaining parts of the mill behind.

May 1970: Johnston Street. Looking down across Ridge Road onto Meanwood Road. The Carr Spinning Mills below date from 1810 and are Grade 2 listed buildings; they are still there at the foot of Buslingthorpe Lane, restored as flats.

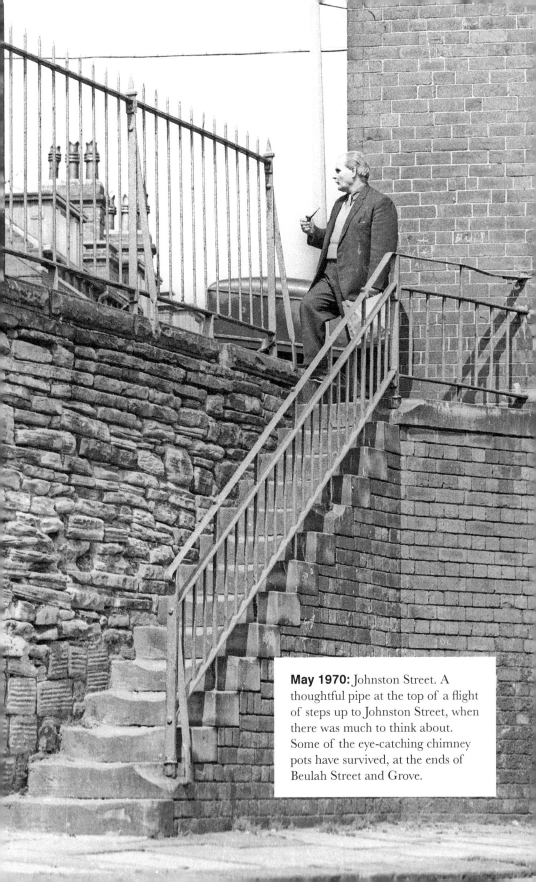

May 1970: Johnston Street. A thoughtful pipe at the top of a flight of steps up to Johnston Street, when there was much to think about. Some of the eye-catching chimney pots have survived, at the ends of Beulah Street and Grove.

Opposite: **April 2023:** Elm Street. Off Johnston Street, this distinctive 'ramp' between street levels with steps at the sides looks just as it did in the 1960s, except that bollards have replaced an iron railing. Beulah Terrace on the left was granted a reprieve in 1978 and Elm Street here marks a demarcation line between what was retained after 1980 and what was redeveloped.

Left: **April 2023:** Johnston Street. Some of the surviving decorative chimney pots at the end of Beulah Grove.

Below: **April 2023:** Johnston Street. The old Chemic Tavern at the end of the street with the end of Beulah Street behind.

July 1968: Thomas Street. Quarry Mount School is at the top, and the street looks much the same today.

August 1996: Quarry Place, Thomas Street's immediate neighbour. This might almost have been taken in 1968 as well, except for the wheelie bins outside the front doors and the later style of lamp post. The plant pots outside the door are an attractive new feature and by this date the residents could breathe a sigh of relief: the policy of wholesale demolition had been discontinued in 1984.

Acknowledgements

Dr Joanne Harrison, for kindly agreeing to write the foreword for us.

The Local and Family History section of Leeds Central Library for their unstinting help: with largescale Ordnance Survey maps of many dates, in finding magazines and periodicals that their index identified for us and for their help with the Baines and Newsome 1834 map of the borough, including permission to reproduce it.

The staff of West Yorkshire Archives Service for access to relevant pre-redevelopment surveys, compulsory purchase orders and other documents, and especially for generous time taken over our email queries about the housing clearances map.

Dalesman Publishing for permission to use the 1980 Rowland Lindup article (see bibliography).

The congregation of All Hallows Church Leeds for their welcome and help.

And everyone who spoke to us in the streets, whether it was to ask what we were doing and pass on snippets of information, or to ask if we needed directions and staying to chat.

Bibliography

(**Abbreviations used in the textual references in square brackets**)

Beresford, Maurice, 'Time and Place: an inaugural lecture on assuming the Chair of Economic History at the University of Leeds' (Leeds University Press, 1961) [Beresford, 1961]

Beresford, Maurice, 'The back-to-back house in Leeds 1787–1939' *Time and Place: Collected Essays* (Hambleton Press, 1985) [Beresford, 1985]

Leach, Peter and Pevsner, Nikolaus, *The Buildings of England: Yorkshire West Riding: Leeds, Bradford and the North* (Yale University Press New Haven and London for The Buildings Books Trust, 2009) [Pevsner, 2009]

Pevsner, Nikolaus and Radcliffe, Enid, *The Buildings of England: Yorkshire West Riding* (Penguin Books Ltd, 1967) [Pevsner, 1967]

Rowley, Allen, and *Yorkshire Evening Post*, *Memory Lane Leeds* Vol. 1 and *Memory Lane Leeds* Vol. 2: *A Second Look* (Derby Books Publishing Co., Derby, 2011)

Waddington-Feather, John, *Leeds: The Heart of Yorkshire: A history and guide to the city and its surroundings* (Basil Jackson Publications, Leeds, 1967) [Waddington-Feather, 1967]

Wrathmell, Susan, *Pevsner Architectural Guides: Leeds* (Yale University Press New Haven and London, 2005) [Wrathmell, 2005]

A1 Street Atlas of Leeds including Pudsey and Horsforth, (Geographia Ltd, London) Date unknown but the edition current October 1967

Articles, Maps, Original Records and Websites

Douglas, Janet, 'Early 19th century working class houses in Leeds', *Victorian Society West Yorkshire Group Journal* (1980), pp.10–12

Lindup, Rowland, 'Life in a Yorkshire Back-to-Back' *Dalesman* (November 1980), pp.658–660 [Lindup, 1980]

Yorkshire Post and *Yorkshire Evening Post*: various dates cited in text [*YP* or *YEP* plus date]

Original Leeds City Council records deposited with the West Yorkshire Archives Service. [WYAS plus reference number]

Map of the Borough of Leeds: Baines and Newsome (1834): reproduced by kind permission of Leeds Libraries

Large scale Ordnance Survey maps [OS plus date as appropriate] and street, trade and telephone directories of various dates from the mid-1800s to the 1970s available in the Local and Family History section of Leeds Central Library

www.littlewoodhouseonline.com

www.secretlibraryleeds.net

www.leodis.net The archive photographs and associated information on Leeds Library and Information Service's Leodis website were a great help in checking the original exact viewpoint of some of Colin's. This useful site provides not only access to their photographic archives but a background information facility, enabling members of the public to add their own comments.

No photographs from any outside source appear in the book: all are copyright Colin M James.

Notes

Introduction

1   *Daily Mirror*, 13 November 1967.

Chapter 1

1   This section is deeply indebted for guidance to the works of Prof. Maurice Beresford as cited in bibliography and also to Janet Douglas' paper 'Early 19th century working class houses in Leeds', *Journal of the West Yorkshire Group of the Victorian Society* (1980), pp.10–12.
2   Beresford, 1985, p.370.
3   Beresford, 1961, p.5.
4   Beresford, 1985, pp.373–4.
5   WYAS LLD1/2/831066: Wellington Road CPO 1960.
6   WYAS LLD1/2/831093/1: Charing Cross and Scott Street CPO March 1954.
7   WYAS LLD1/2/11831170.
8   Pevsner (1967), p.337.
9   Pevsner 1967, p 337.
10   WYAS 1869: In the Leeds City Council Housing Department Environmental Health Section Records. Based on an earlier map repurposed. We are grateful to WYAS for sorting out later confusion over its identity.
11   WYAS LC/HE/3879/3/2: Woodhouse (Rider Road) Clearance Order (Part) CPO 1980: background paper for public inquiry: source of much useful information regarding housing redevelopment project.
12   WYAS LLD74/3/54/10.
13   Beresford, 1961, p.5.
14   Eg WYAS LLD1/2/831066: Wellington Road CPO, 1960.
15   www.leodis.net search by entering 'Quarry Hill Flats'.
16   Shown as empty on the 1960s map plate 01.

Chapter 2

1   Edward Baines and Son were the printers and publishers of the 1834 Directory of Leeds (and the *Leeds Mercury* newspaper), with which the map may well have appeared. Reid Newsome was a bookseller at the same address: 149 Briggate. (Information supplied by the Local History Library at Leeds Central Library.)
2   See colour plate 04.
3   Cast iron posts, rather like mileposts, with this date on were erected to mark the boundary.
4   Beresford, 1985, p.367.
5   General Wade's 1745 camp should not be confused with that of General Fairfax during the Civil War, which was on Woodhouse Moor itself.
6   Beresford, 1985, p.376.
7   OS 1893.
8   No longer in existence.
9   Grosvenor Hill ascended immediately alongside Servia Hill but ended at a factory and barely exists today. As a result it is not named on the 1960s street map. It is important here, however, because several photographs show it.
10 *YEP*, 5 April 2007.
11 *YEP*, 11 Dec 1969.
12 WYAS LLD1/1/A14358.
13 WYAS LLD1/2/835290/1 Woodhouse (Institution Street) Clearance Area 1-5 CPO 1967.
14 WYAS LLD1/2/815937 Johnston Street Area papers.
15 Lindup, 1980, p.660.
16 WYAS LLD1/2/837905 (among Oatland Lane/Bristol Road papers).
17 WYAS LLD1/2/815937 Johnson Street Area papers.
18 *YEP*, 11 December 1969.

Chapter 3

1   Wrathmell, 2005, p.188, quoting the Leeds historian Ralph Thoresby.
2   WYAS 1869.
3   Much fascinating information on this area appeared in the Little Woodhouse Neighbourhood Design Statement, 2011, prepared for Little Woodhouse Community Association by Peter LH Baker RIBA MRTPI IHBC Their website is www.littlewoodhouseonline.com
4   *YEP*, 5 December 1969.
5   WYAS LLD1/2/840760 Westfield Road (Rosebank View) Clearance Area 12 (part) 305 CPO 1969.
6   Pevsner, 2009, p.486.
7   *YEP*, 5 December 1969.
8   Pevsner, 2009, p.486.

Chapter 4

1   Lindup, Rowland, 'Life in a Yorkshire Back-to-Back' *Dalesman* (November 1980), pp.658–660. Rowland Lindup was a talented artist and began the long-running series of 'Old Amos' drawings and sayings in *The Dalesman*, continued after his death in 1989 to the present by his son Peter Lindup. See *Dalesman* (May 2023), pp.27–29: article marking the seventieth anniversary of the first 'Old Amos' drawing.
2   Probably the 1920s and '30s.
3   *YEP*, 24 December 1983.
4   WYAS LLD1/2/40882 Woodhouse (Jubilee Road) Clearance Area CPO 1971.

Chapter 5

1   *YEP*, 8 February 1973, p.6.
2   Waddington-Feather, 1967, pp.121–2.
3   *YEP*, 23 February 1973.
4   Leeds City Transport prices were very good, compared to our buses at home: in 1967 you could get into town from the university for 2d!
5   Lindup, 1980, p.660.

Chapter 6

1   WYAS LLD1/2/837905 Oatland Lane/Bristol Road papers.
2   Beresford, 1985, p.366.
3   Called Lavinia Street on maps, this street always appears in the contemporary records spelt Livinia as is today's namesake Livinia Grove.
4   Information on this pub appears on the internet at www.secretleeds.com

Chapter 7

1   Text-author's observations working in a local museum in the 1970s and '80s.
2   *YEP*, 8 February 1973, p.6.
3   *YEP*, 16 December 1980.
4   WYAS LC/HE/3879/3/2: Paper prepared for the Inquiry arising from the Woodhouse (Rider Road) Clearance Area (part) compulsory purchase order 1980. The useful background summary forms a major source of information for this chapter.
5   WYAS LLD8/2/2/6/2: Woodhouse (Rider Road) Clearance Area papers OBJ 21.
6   *YEP*, 16 December 1980.
7   In 1970 we went to a 'pre-demolition' party in a house in Oswald Terrace in Leeds 12 that had a plumbed-in bath in that position.
8   WYAS LLD8/2/2/6/2: Woodhouse (Rider Road) Clearance Area papers.
9   WYAS LLD1/2/831066: Wellington Road CPO 1960 (includes Johnston Street).

10 *YEP*, 31 January 2021. Feature on nine unusual pub names in Leeds.

11 SAVE was created in 1975 by a group of journalists, historians, architects, and planners to campaign publicly for endangered historic buildings. It is also active on the broader issues of preservation policy.

12 *YP*, 5 November 1981, p.14.

13 *YEP*, 17 February 1977, p.18.

14 There were many other factors, social and political, local and national, which fed into this transition in overall thinking, which we feel go beyond the remit of this book, and the limitations on local research opportunities placed upon its authors. Some demolition still happens: notably the Garnets in Leeds 11 in 2012.

15 *Yorkshire Weekend Post*, 28 December 1985, p.11.

16 WYAS LLD1/2/840826 Woodhouse (Bagby Fields) Clearance Area Compulsory Purchase Order 1970.

Index

Note: Page numbers of images are in italics; colour plates are indicated with a 'C' and are in bold.